52 tips
to increase
Total Revenue

Written by
Ronny F. Sandvik

About the author

Ronny F. Sandvik was born in Bodø, Norway.

He has his education from the Norwegian Army, the University of Tromsø, the Norwegian School of Management and Business Administration (Bergen, Norway), and Hautes Etudes Commerciales (Paris, France). His work experience is from the Norwegian Army (food supply), The Boston Consulting Group (strategy), the grocery chain ICA (marketing, category management), Cultivator (sales and negotiation skills), and Anker STI (Finance, Marketing and IT).

While writing this book (in 2018), the author worked as the CFO at Anker STI (hotel, hostel, student apartments, parking, offices and stores).

See www.anker.oslo.no for more information about this company.

For more information about the author, please look at:
www.linkedin.com/in/ronnyfredriksandvik
www.facebook.com/ronny.sandvik

Please also visit this Facebook page:
www.facebook.com/practicalhotelmanagement

Chapters   Page

Chapter 1: General tips

Tip number 1: Technology

There are many IT systems, booking engines, booking platforms, channel managers, PMS's, GDS's, website platforms, integration technology etc. Make sure you understand the choices you have, but be confident when you have decided. You can earn money in different ways, if you have functional technology in your company.
The rest of the tips in this book can be adjusted to whatever system you use.
Therefore, tip number one is to put away the technology choices for a moment, and try to understand the potential in the tips described in this book.

Tip number 2: Structure

Make sure you have a standard rate for every date the next calendar year. This is the rate you use if the date acts normal, meaning it will neither be a peak demand nor a low occupancy date. This starting rate should be communicated to your colleagues as a list price they can use if no new rate is distributed. A part of this planning is to make seasonal variance in rates. Make sure you at least know when it will be high and low season, maybe you also would like to include a mid-season. Typically, you will end up with 5-10 date periods throughout the year. Remember to also consider day-of-week pricing, having different rates in weekends vs mid-week.

Tip number 3: Prognoses

Make prognoses of how many guest nights, how many room nights (occupancy rate) and which average daily rate you expect per month for the next calendar year. As time goes, measure real performance and compare it to the prognoses you made earlier. In this way, you will learn the natural variance of occupancy in your area/city, and you will improve your ability to make good prognoses in the future. Most hotels will also make a daily forecast for every month. Such detailed prognoses can be used internally to plan the need for staff in various departments. A good prognosis routine can have an additional positive effect, it will highlight periods which will underperform, forcing you to act to avoid this.

Tip number 4: Channels are different

Different sales channels have different campaign possibilities. This is mainly because they use technology with certain constraints, or they built up the system with a certain logic. Therefore, make sure you understand the particularities with each channel. One type of campaign can give a boost in one channels, while it's not possible in the other. It also means that one logic across all channels seldom is possible. Make sure you play around in every extranet, trying to understand both the possibilities and the constraints.

Tip number 5: Function > Title

"do you have a Revenue Manager" they say… It doesn't matter whether the responsible is the Sales Manager, the Director of Marketing, the Booking Manager, or a person with the title Revenue Manager. The important is that the revenue function is taken care of. That means that everyone knows who's responsible for the revenue management, the one who optimize all revenue. This person should have enough time and competence to go deep into the subject so that the function is well taken care of. There are a lot of courses to attend, industry experts to interview, books and articles to read, industry magazines to follow. A strong understanding of mathematics and good skills in statistics will make it easier to perform when you are responsible for the revenue in a company.

Tip number 6: Many people involved

The Revenue Management should be a task performed by many people. In the previous tip, we stressed the importance of having one responsible for the function. Normally, it would be very vulnerable to have only one person optimizing revenue. This person should aim to include others in the task. The result would be even better decisions, more actions performed, and less actions missed. In most hotels, actions are missed when the revenue responsible is on vacation, on sick leave, on seminar/conference, or busy with other projects/tasks. Revenue Management should be learned by all relevant employees working with management, sale, booking, reception, conference, restaurant, bar. With such a strategy, the entire organization will contribute to the Total Revenue.

Tip number 7: The Product

Before you decide on your standard rates, evaluate your main product: the hotel room. Which level of quality are you offering to the customers? Is that a level in line with your strategy? Are all the hotel rooms at the same level of quality? Is there a large spread in how the guests will experience the product? You may want to adjust your pricing if you have a product that differs a lot. One way to do that is to create different room categories according to standard so that you can have a more thrust worthy presentation of your rooms. This will also ensure that the guests paying most will get the best rooms, leading to higher satisfaction and better reviews.

Tip number 8: The daily rate communicated

Make sure that when you have adjusted rates at a given date, all people knows how to find that updated rate. If you have revenue management centralized, you need an easy system so that all booking and reception employees know where to find the correct price. Normally this will be updated in a calendar in your IT system, where everyone can look up the daily rate. Also think about how you want your colleagues to explain why a rate varies according to date. If explained in a nice and honest way, guests tend to accept the nature of dynamic pricing. A typical way of telling this in an honest and direct way is: There are only a few rooms left in the city, therefore every hotel take a higher rate for those last rooms.

Chapter 2: Low season tips

Tip 9: Early bookings

Make an early booking campaign where you give a discount to guests booking 30 days before arrival. By crediting people who make plans, you can take a higher part of those cost oriented and price sensitive guests. You will reduce risk by getting bookings into the calendar early. If you want an even stronger campaign, you can make the rule less strict by reducing the number of days to 20. To ensure that you don't sell to cheap, you should limit the stay dates for the campaign, normally you will not include high season and special events.

Tip 10: Long Stay

Make a long stay campaign where you give a discount to guests staying more than 2/3/4/5/10 days. There is a trend towards having many levels of long stay, meaning you get a higher discount the longer you stay. Examples can be: 10 % if you stay 2 nights, 20 % if you stay 3 nights, 25 % if you stay 4 nights, etc. Apartment hotels usually have rules with even longer stays: "Minimum 2 weeks, pay 100 USD per night". Longer stays give less administration for your hotel team, and is truly an important element to optimize revenue.

Tip 11: Non-refundable

Make a non-refundable campaign where you give a discount to guests that agrees to a no cancellation rule. People change plans all the time, and with all the booking engines available today, they tend to shop around even after they have booked. Given them a discount makes them satisfied with the rate, stopping them from trying to find an even better deal. It will reduce administration regarding cancellations, and it will give you important safe bookings in the calendar.

Tip 12: Free nights

Get more bookings by giving the 4th night for free. The important thing for you is to get many arrivals to ensure a certain level of room nights. At the same time, the cost of giving the 4th night is low if you have available rooms. The guest will save 25 % during the stay, increasing the probability that your hotel will be chosen. Such guests also give the opportunity to sell food & beverage in the bar/restaurant, since guests spend more time in the hotel.

Tip 13: Flash sale

If you have a period in your low season where you barely receive any booking, a flash sale may be the answer. Giving a limited-time discount will give a ranking boost in the chosen sales channels. One week booking window can give you a significant amount of bookings for the coming months. Just make sure that you only include stay dates where you can afford to give a discount (exclude high season).

Tip 14: Last minute

Giving a discount to late bookers can be an efficient way of filling those last rooms. Some channels even specialize in this way of selling rooms. If you load availability at a compatible price, it can give you increased visibility among tourists arriving your district without having a pre-booked hotel. There is a trend in this segment where people book last minute rooms on their mobile devices. This can become a large segment, and you want your fair share. However, you don't want to teach all customers to book close to arrival, therefore you should only use last minute campaigns occasionally.

Tip 15: Members only

Many sales channels have a club of preferred customers. It can be members of a bonus program, newsletter subscribers, booking geniuses (booked a certain number of times) or other chosen customers. Giving a discount to this club of people can ensure that you communicate with people more likely to book. It is often called a secret deal because only the members see it (and hopefully your competitors will not see it). Make sure to evaluate whether such discounts give you extra bookings, and not just lower rate on bookings you would have received anyway.

Tip 16: Social media campaign

If you have followers on your FB page, on your Instagram profile, or on other social media, you can reward them by giving a discount only communicated in that media. By doing this correctly, you can increase the number of followers, since people will tell their friends about the benefit of following your hotel. You also ensure that they book directly with you, meaning you don't have to pay any provision. Social media can build a closer relationship to your customers, and it is a good place to communicate news about your hotel and interesting happenings in the area surrounding it.

Tip 17: Adjusting rate down

Often you will see that one date is less popular than the days before and after. It can be a Sunday, when the weekend guests have checked out and the business guests have not yet arrived. It can also be a date between two events in your district. When you have such a date with less occupancy and you don't want to lose the shoulder dates, you can adjust down the rate for the least popular date. Hopefully this will give you longer stays that include the least popular date, and it will increase your market share among guests staying only that date.

Tip 18: Pick the right mix of tools

When you sit down to load the different kind of campaigns you sometimes feel unsure whether it's necessary to have these campaigns or not. When it's difficult to decide, I bet that the best choice is something in between. Campaign or not? Do it for some room types! Do it for some dates! Do it with less % discount! Make the rule strict instead of no campaign!
As always, the answer is not black or white…

Chapter 3: High season tips

Tip 19: Increase the rates

When high season gets closer you often see that the high season rates you made some months ago, are too low. You should have an alarm that buzzes if a high season date fills up too early. The solution is easy, increase the rate that day, and evaluate all other dates in the same period. The most common mistakes in dynamic pricing are: forgetting to increase, forgetting to increase once more, increasing to late, increasing to little, having a max rate which is too low. Increasing rates is a mental process where you need to challenge your thoughts about how much a hotel room is worth. Remember that it's voluntary for the guest to book the room, they have no reason to complain if they get what you presented.

Tip 20: Long stay rule

If one date peaks much more than the ones before/after, make a long stay rule on the popular date to make sure you benefit on the shoulder dates as well. If not, the day before or after risk low occupancy. The result is that the rest of the bookings on the most popular date are at least a 2-night stay (you decide how strict the long stay rule should be). This is a powerful tool that ensures longer stays and less administration in a busy high season period. Make sure you also use this rule when selling more manually; on the phone, via email and in the reception.

Tip 21: The popular room type

Evaluate the rate gap between single, twin, triple and family room. Do you have a period where for some reason, the family rooms always sell out first? That means they could have been sold at a higher rate. You probably have a rule within your hotel that a triple cost x more than the twin, and a family room cost x more than a triple. In certain periods, go beyond that rule and increase the rate for that third and fourth person. This will give you that extra increase on the ADR.

Tip 22: The double used as single

During business dates, you need to upgrade many guests so that there are only 1 guest in rooms with more beds. You can try to force that business person to pay the higher rate since it's a larger room, but that is often difficult. A different and maybe better strategy is to upsell the larger room to the guest by pricing it higher than a single, but slightly lower than a double/twin. This can give you more guests than the neighbour hotel, especially when it's not a 100 % occupancy date. If it's a peak date in high season, you will of course charge as a double/twin/triple/quad even if it's only 1 person.

Tip 23: Selling without commission

Some sales persons are not responsible for costs. In those cases, they will not reflect on how much it cost to sell a room in different channels. In the hotel industry, it's common to pay 5-25 % commission, depending on the channel. Even at your own webpage, where most people would think there is zero cost, it is often some percentages to pay for the technology behind the booking engine. With all this in mind, it may very well be clever to sell the last and most expensive rooms by phone, by email or in the reception. The revenue may not go up, but the result after cost will improve.

Tip 24: Forced cross sale

Some peak dates you want to guarantee that you get income from other categories than hotel rooms. During this period, you only sell rack rate rooms to guests that also buy other services. This could be a conference package, preferably with both a day package and a dinner. It could also be an event in your summer garden, such as a wedding party. Such "forced" cross sale can feel strict, but it's all about finding the customer that see the value in the total service. For instance, the wedding guests often pay only for the room, while the bride and groom pay for the event. In such cases, the forced cross sale will not be experienced very strict by the guests.

Tip 25: Testing the max price

Occasionally there are some dates where the city is completely booked. On such dates, you can take much higher rates than you think. If a hotel normally charges 100 for a single room, they tend to have a Rack rate (the highest they go) at around 200. This is the old-fashioned way of doing it. The new trend is to have no max rate, instead you try to set new records. In this way, you will challenge your mindset and move from "no I cannot charge that much" to "but of course it's worth 500 to get the last room in town". Remember: it is voluntary to book that last room, and the customer often must compare it to the cost of staying in a different area (increased travel cost to the meeting), and to the cost of changing date/cancelling (not attending the important conference).

Tip 26: Selling the last rooms one by one

When you only have a few rooms left and you realize that this is a date where people are willing to pay much for the last rooms: don't put all the rest of the rooms out for sale at once. A typical mistake is a hotel where you think 200 USD is a high rate, and you load all the available rooms at that rate level. You will risk that they sell out very quickly at a good rate, but not at a VERY good rate. First you can sell 5 rooms at 200, if that goes very quickly, you load 5 more rooms at 250, and you evaluate whether that is an acceptable rate level for the market that day. If it's too high, you lower it to 220. If it's acceptable, you try 280. If you use robots to adjust rates, you must assure that they are programmed to think this way.

Tip 27: High rates from long term partners

Most hotels have some long-term partners who get special negotiated rates due to frequency of arrivals, volume of stays, sponsorships etc. With such clients, it will feel uncomfortable refusing them to stay at a certain date, or to charge them higher than the normal rate. The solution is to explain them early in the relationship that special dates can be more expensive. If you use formal contracts, these should include such rules. It will also be a good solution to give them a good discount from the rack rate, still much higher than the normal rate.

Chapter 4: Restaurant tips

Tip 28: The online booking

Sometimes it can be difficult to be available on the phone at all hours. With an online booking solution, you ensure that the modern restaurant guest get an immediate confirmation on his booking. This will increase number of guests and may be worth it even if you need to pay some provision. Many online booking solutions are very professional, giving guests not only confirmations, but reminders so that no show probability is reduced. Instead of using a lot of money to build your own booking solutions, benchmark which ones exist already, and be part of that one. In this way, you will automatically benefit from new versions, and incremental improvements. Make sure you use the online booking actively, loading enough availability, updating it often.

Tip 29: The table combinations

Try to offer many table combinations so that guests with different preferences find their ideal table. One restaurant can have: 10 tables with 2 guests, 5 tables with 4 guests, 2 round tables with 6 guests, one long table where you mix different people/groups. The best is if you can easily adjust the table combinations according to time of day and the actual demand in every moment. Professional waiters move tables often to optimize the number of seatings. Think about this already when you decide which tables to purchase.

Tip 30: The wardrobe dilemma

Sometimes when guest arrive to the restaurant, they bring a lot of shopping bags, purses, and their outdoor clothes. There should be enough coat stands, wall pegs and other wardrobe alternatives so that the guest easily can settle down. If not, you risk that 2 guests occupy 4-6 seats, making it impossible to serve as many guests as you want to. You often see people coming in the front door to look for a table, then they turn around and disappear. Not all waiters have the trained eye to understand that they turned around because of the seat occupied by a shopping bag.

Tip 31: The menu

Create a menu with logical sections: starters, mains, desserts, beer, wine, other drinks, non-alcoholic drinks. Try to make it easy for the guest to separate the sections, remember that people tend to read a menu from left to right, from top to bottom. Making it to creative can make it harder to understand. Use fonts and layout that makes it easy to read. Having many choices of food to impress the guests can sometimes make it harder to decide, and can also make the menu less reliable. How is it possible to make so many dishes? A well designed (and proofread) menu can boost your sales.

Tip 32: The special menu

There are some dates where you know that the restaurant will be fully booked. It may be the national day, the New Year's Eve, or a different kind of celebration in your district. In these occasions, it may be worth it to make a special "Menu of the day". Such a menu should make the administration easier for you, and the profit much larger. You simply present fewer choices than normal (often more exclusive dishes) and price them higher. A normal way of selling more is to only sell 3-course menus that day. Remember, don't be fanatic, you may want to make exceptions to ensure that families and guests with special wishes are happy when they leave.

Tip 33: The service

People who dine & wine often have certain expectations when they arrive to a restaurant. They want to be greeted with a welcome of some kind. They want to understand whether this is a restaurant where you wait to be seated or choose a table yourself. When they sit down, they want some free water as soon as possible, together with a menu. Train your waiters to scan the room so that they see when the guests are ready to order. It is cool when a waiter remembers every detail a large group has ordered, but get realistic, use pen & paper. It creates trust and reduces stress for both customer (will the waiter remember that special need?) and waiter (I wrote all down, now I can concentrate on scanning the room for other guests trying to contact me).

Tip 34: The food trends

Tip 34: make good food! That must be the most important, but remember to monitor the latest trends in the society. People want healthy food. That doesn't mean they stop eating red meat, but you can help them by reducing the size of the steak and adding more vegetables. Your menu can emphasize and suggest fish and vegetable options. The amount of salt can be reduced significantly by adding other flavor enhancements. You can contribute to food waste reduction by using smaller plates and serving suitable portions. Even offering doggy bags is a trend coming to more and more restaurants. Monitor trends constantly and adjust how you prepare the food.

Tip 35: Upselling at the end of the meal

All sales oriented waiters know that selling dessert and/or coffee at the end of the meal will increase the results. Purchase cost on such ingredients is low, sales income is high, hence the margin is high. All employees should be trained in upselling so that every bill gets as high as it can be. The only exception is when there's a long queue of people waiting for a table. In such cases, it may be wise to being less pushy on the last cup of coffee, to ensure that you not lose the potential next bill (people who leaves the queue before they get a table).

Tip 36: The bill

Sometimes you are happy with the waiter and the food, you are in a good mood, you want to leave to reach your next appointment, and you don't get the bill. You don't even get the chance to ask for the bill, because all the waiters are busy welcoming other guests. Remember that the restaurant experience lasts until the guest leave the premises. Many guests will reduce the gratuity because of the long waiting time to pay the bill. Train all waiters to scan the restaurant to notice guests who try to contact them.

Chapter 5: Bar tips

Tip 37: Online info about the bar

Make sure you inform all potential guests about the existence of your bar. Some guests will make sure that they book a hotel with a proper bar, therefore it's essential that you include information on your webpage and in all online sales channels. Good information will include a picture, opening hours and a description of what you sell. In some countries, it's legal to invite guests to a welcome drink in the bar, making them familiar with the bar for the rest of the stay. In others, such pushy sales techniques must be avoided to ensure that all laws are followed.

Tip 38: Offline info about the bar

When guests arrive, you want to ensure that they know where the bar is situated. This is very easy if the bar is next to the reception, but in many cases, you need to explain how to find it. Information can be given from the receptionists, but you may also consider having information in elevators, in all guest rooms, and at other relevant places in the hotel. The bar is a good place for guests to gather before they go out for dinner, and they will remember it for the nightcap.

Tip 39: The bar concept

Try to attract bar guests by creating a nice visual impression of the bar. Make sure to have good lighting so that the bar area invites you to enter. Present the selection of beverages by showing the bottles on shelves at the wall behind the bar counter. Create a nice style by choosing furniture's and art that fit together. Give the bar a name that tells something about the concept, and creates a feeling of atmosphere. If you are unhappy with your bar concept today, take an inspection round in popular bars and hotels, to gather inspiration.

Tip 40: Comfortable seating

It is important that bar guests want to stay for that second drink. Make sure you have comfortable chairs and sofas, with tables suited for the chosen seating. Make sure you have a good mix of sections, so that both individuals, couples and groups find a place to chill. Some cool bar stools are a must in a professional bar. This is where the lonely traveler can sit down and chat with the bartender, and with other guests.

Chapter 6: Conference tips

Tip 41: Dynamic pricing on meeting rooms

Historically, most hotels have a list of prices per conference room per day/hour. To optimize revenue in the conference department, you need to use dynamic pricing on meeting rooms as you do with hotel rooms. If you know it will be a busy date in the conference segment, you should increase the rates on some/all meeting rooms. As a start, you may want to change the rate list: until now you have been giving a fixed rate, in the future you indicate a rate span from x to y. You simply tell customers that on certain dates, conference rooms are higher priced because of high demand.

Tip 42: Customer price sensitivity

If you want a good mix of customers from different segment, you should try to understand their needs, their willingness to pay the rate you demand. Instead of making it a "take it or leave it" decision, you should be open to classify certain clients as low-budget/charity/culture/youth. These are customers that may have the opportunity to rent meeting rooms at odd hours, where you don't have that many business clients. Giving such a discount can also make the word spread to similar groups of people, giving you even higher sales.

Tip 43: Upselling the best meeting room

One way to sell at higher rates is to highlight unique features to your best meeting rooms: "our rate that day for 20 people is 1000, but if you put in 200 more, I can reserve our best room with view to the river instead of normal city view, what do you think?" Other unique features can be: higher under the ceiling, more spacious, separate coffee machine, better chairs, more modern technique etc. People are more willing to accept higher rates if they feel that they get something in return for the extra money.

Tip 44: Finding the extra meeting room

Are you sure you have only 7 meeting rooms? How about the garden, the corner in the lobby, the extra-large hotel room, the lounge, the restaurant, the bar? If all the conference rooms in the neighbourhood are occupied, and you explain thoroughly and honestly to the customer, you may be able to sell an extra meeting room on certain dates. If they are well informed, they often tend to find such meeting spaces exciting and interesting to experience. Try it once and evaluate: which rules should be applied for this space in terms of equipment available, possible hours, which clients etc.

Tip 45: Day rate vs half-day rate

If you rent out a room several times a day, you should be compensated due to the extra preparation, service, cleaning and administration. A daily rate of 1000 can be divided into 2 half-day rates of 700, or 3 three-hour meetings of 600 each. The more arrivals in a conference room on a day, the more total revenue that day. When you understand the need of your regular clients, it is easier to optimize by dividing the calendar into the best blocks.

Tip 46: Bundling issues: VAT

Many hotels offer a Full Board Meeting Package, which includes accommodation, breakfast, lunch, dinner, meeting room participation, and 2 coffee breaks with snack/cake/fruit. When they do, they include a discount since the customer buys many things. Be aware of the VAT: if food and beverage have a different tax rate than accommodation and meeting room, you as a hotel are interested to keep the F & B part of the package as low as possible. At the same time, the restaurant needs to earn money so that the tax authorities are happy.

Tip 47: Bundling issues: ADR

When offering a Full Board Meeting Package, you usually have decided how much of the list price goes to: 1. the hotel room, 2. the meeting room, 3. the restaurant (divided into breakfast, lunch, coffee breaks and dinner). The challenge is what to do when you offer a 10 % discount to the package, do you give 10 % on all 3, or do you give it only on one of them. Some hotels feel that the restaurant needs a fixed rate to survive, so the risk should be on the hotel room. Therefore, Average Daily Rate fluctuates depending on which rate the package achieved. It may not be a problem since dynamic pricing on hotel rooms are well adapted, but we aware of this effect on ADR. An alternative can be to give the risk to the meeting room, having a predefined discount distribution, or to bundle without discounts.

Tip 48: Day package vs room+food

In a day package priced at 700, you may have a distribution of 300 to the meeting room and 400 to the restaurant. Let's say you offer two choices to the customer, either day package at 700 or room only at 10 000. That means that a clever customer can calculate that if they are 34 people (10 000/300) or more, they could benefit by renting the room plus food, instead of the day package per person. It is crucial that sales persons have a deep understanding of this, to be able to optimize and respond to clever clients. It is important that you get as high total revenue as possible, without making the customer feel tricked.

Chapter 7: Final remarks

Tip 49: Product development

Remember that your hotel gets worn down constantly. Every guest will make a small scratch that reduces the impression of the room. As a sales person, you must always contribute to a steady renovation pace, making it easier to accomplish good reviews. Constant surveillance of trends, new technology and innovation is a precondition to ensure long term growth. Learn from the best, be curious on all new hotel openings, benchmark with your competitors. Product is one of the original 4 P's in the marketing mix (Product, Price, Place, Promotion), and should be a focus in the sales department.

Tip 50: Pictures and videos

Famous last words: we already have pictures, why do you ask us to take new ones? The pace of technology improvement is high and increasing. Pictures should have more pixels than before to look good on new platforms, guests want to see the product before they decide. If you lack a picture of the bathroom, they instantly suspect that you're embarrassed by it. Special features in your hotel should be presented by a recently made video, with high standard. 360 degree views are more and more common, and will soon be a commodity. Make sure to include photo cost in every budget.

Tip 51: Find that extra sale channel

Due to potential commission, there is a high degree of innovation regarding how a hotel room is sold to the end customer. Modern high-tech websites can invest more than a hotel chain, giving them the best customer experience. Other tour operators specialize in niche markets, such as tailor-made trips, high end customers, eco-friendly experiences, child friendly hotels etc. Ensure that you are updated on this development and try a new channel regularly. Keep the ones that perform, kick out the ones who don't. Use this thinking not only for the hotel rooms, but also for the restaurant, the bar and the conference department.

Tip 52: Choose your 5 favorite tips

Hopefully you found some interesting tips in this book. Each one invites you to dig deeper into the subject. The last advice is to read the tips once more to get a better overview of the total thinking. You will probably find some of them obvious, others irrelevant. Are you sure that your key colleagues have the same understanding? You can give them one tip each and ask them to prepare a workshop where they present how your hotel perform in that area. Choose a few tips where you have improvement potential, and work with these.

All the best!